Swe
PIES AND
PUDDINGS

Your Promise of Success

Welcome to the world of Confident Cooking, created for you in
our test kitchen, where recipes are double tested by our team
of home economists to achieve a high standard of success.

MURDOCH BOOKS
Sydney • London • Vancouver

Sweet pies

Reacquaint yourself with the not-so-humble pie. Whether you fancy the hearty country charm of a traditional shortcrust apple pie or the European touch of filo pastry, these sweet pies, tarts and strudels will keep you happy. Ring the changes by taking advantage of plentiful seasonal fruits and, for a completely indulgent end to your meal, accompany dessert with a dollop of sweetened mascarpone flavoured with liqueur.

Pumpkin Pie

Preparation time:
  20 minutes + 30 minutes standing time
Cooking time:
  40 minutes
Serves 8

1 1/4 cups plain flour
100 g butter, chopped
2 teaspoons caster sugar
4 tablespoons water, chilled
1 egg yolk, lightly beaten
1 tablespoon milk

Filling
2 eggs, lightly beaten
3/4 cup soft brown sugar
500 g pumpkin, cooked, mashed and cooled
1/3 cup cream
1 tablespoon sherry

1 teaspoon ground cinnamon
1/2 teaspoon ground nutmeg
1/2 teaspoon ground ginger

1 Preheat oven to moderate 180°C. Sift flour into large mixing bowl; add chopped butter. Using fingertips, rub the butter into the flour for 2 minutes or until the mixture is a fine, crumbly texture; stir in sugar. Add almost all the liquid, mix to a firm dough, adding more liquid if necessary. Turn onto a lightly floured surface, knead for 1 minute or until smooth. Store, covered with plastic wrap, in refrigerator for at least 30 minutes.

Pumpkin Pie (top), Anzac Apple Tart (bottom).

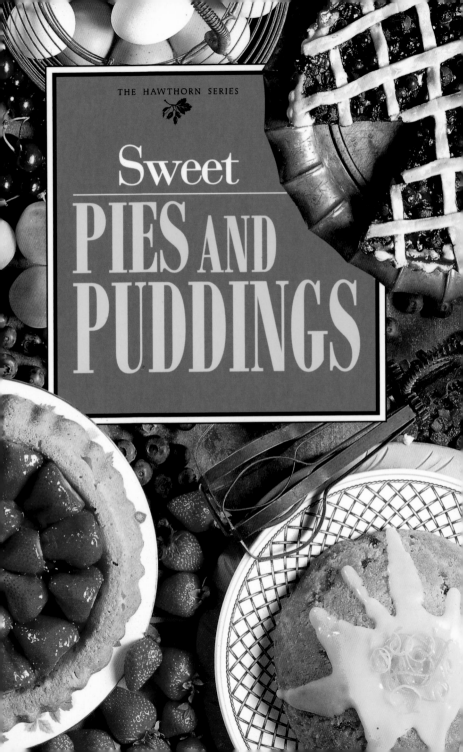

THE HAWTHORN SERIES

Sweet
PIES AND
PUDDINGS

USEFUL INFORMATION

Easy	A little care needed	More care needed

All our recipes are thoroughly tested in our test kitchen. Standard metric measuring cups and spoons approved by Standards Australia are used in the development of our recipes. All cup and spoon measurements are level. We have used eggs with an average weight of 60 g each in all recipes. Can sizes vary from manufacturer to manufacturer and between countries; use the can size closest to the one suggested in the recipe.

Australian Metric Cup and Spoon Measures

For dry ingredients the standard set of metric measuring cups consists of 1 cup, ½ cup, ⅓ cup and ¼ cup sizes.

For measuring liquids, a transparent, graduated measuring jug is available in either a 250 mL cup or a 1 litre jug.

The basic set of metric spoons, used to measure both dry and liquid ingredients, is made up of 1 tablespoon, 1 teaspoon, ½ teaspoon and ¼ teaspoon.

British and American Cup and Spoon Conversion

Australian	British/American
1 tablespoon	3 teaspoons
2 tablespoons	¼ cup
¼ cup	⅓ cup
⅓ cup	½ cup
½ cup	⅔ cup
⅔ cup	¾ cup
¾ cup	1 cup
1 cup	1¼ cups

Oven Temperatures

Electric	C	F
Very Slow	120	250
Slow	150	300
Mod Slow	160	325
Moderate	180	350
Mod Hot	210	425
Hot	240	475
Very Hot	260	525

Gas	C	F
Very Slow	120	250
Slow	150	300
Mod Slow	160	325
Moderate	180	350
Mod Hot	190	375
Hot	200	400
Very Hot	230	450

Glossary

capsicum = sweet pepper
eggplant = aubergine
zucchini = courgettes

Published by Murdoch Books, a division of Murdoch Magazines Pty Ltd. 213 Miller Street, North Sydney, NSW 2060 **Manager Food Publications:** Jo Anne Calabria. **Home Economists:** Kerrie Ray, Tracy Rutherford. **Editor:** Rosalie Higson. **Design and Finished Art:** Annette Fitzgerald. **Photographer:** Hans Schlupp. **Step Photographer:** Reg Morrison. **Food Stylist:** Georgina Dolling. **Food Stylist's Assistant:** Jodie Vassallo. **Publisher:** Anne Wilson. **Publishing Manager:** Mark Newman. **Production Manager:** Catie Ziller. **Marketing Manager:** Mark Smith. **National Sales Manager:** Keith Watson. National Library of Australia. Cataloguing-in-Publication Data. Sweet Pies and Pudding. Includes index. ISBN 0 86411 310.2 1.Pies. 2.Cookery (Puddings) 641.864. First published 1993. Printed by Toppan Printing Co. Ltd, Singapore. Typeset by Adtype, North Sydney. ©Murdoch Books 1993. All rights reserved. No part of this publication may be reproduced, stored in any retrieval system or transmitted in any form or by any means electronic, mechanical, photocopying, recording or otherwise without the prior written permission of the publisher. Murdoch Books is a trade mark of Murdoch Magazines Pty Ltd. Distributed in UK by Australian Consolidated Press (UK) Ltd, 20 Galowhill Road, Brackmills, Northampton NN4 OEE. Enquiries – 0604 760456

The Publisher thanks the following for their assistance in the photography of this book: Hale Imports; Porters Limewash; Seconds Out; Wardlaw Fabrics; Waterford Wedgwood; Villeroy & Boch; All Sydney. 1908 Tearooms; Tasmania.

2 Roll out the pastry between 2 sheets of plastic wrap, large enough to cover base and sides of 23 cm pie dish; reserve the pastry trimmings. Roll out the trimmings to 2 mm thickness and, using a sharp knife, cut into leaf shapes of different sizes. Score vein markings onto leaves. Beat egg yolk with milk, and brush onto pastry edge. Arrange leaves around pastry edge, pressing gently to attach. Brush leaves lightly with egg mixture.
3 Cut a sheet of greaseproof paper large enough to cover the pastry-lined dish. Spread a layer of dried beans or rice evenly over paper. Bake for 10 minutes, remove from oven and discard paper and beans. Return pastry to oven for 5 minutes or until it is lightly golden. Set aside to cool.
4 To make Filling: Whisk the eggs and sugar in a large mixing bowl. Add pumpkin, cream, sherry and spices and combine thoroughly. Pour into pastry shell and bake for 40 minutes or until set. If pastry edge begins to brown too much during cooking, cover with aluminium foil. Serve at room temperature.

Anzac Apple Tart
Preparation time:
  15 minutes + 30
  minutes standing time
Cooking time:
  30 minutes
Serves 6

1 cup plain flour
75 g butter, chopped
1 egg yolk, lightly
  beaten
1 tablespoon water,
  chilled

Filling
1¼ cups rolled oats
¼ cup caster sugar
½ cup plain flour
100 g butter
2 tablespoons golden
  syrup
1 x 410 g can pie apple

1 Preheat oven to moderate 180°C. Sift flour into a large mixing bowl; add chopped butter. Using fingertips, rub butter into flour for 2 minutes or until mixture is a fine, crumbly texture. Add egg yolk and almost all the water, mix to a firm dough,

adding more water if necessary. Turn onto a lightly floured surface, knead 1 minute or until smooth. Store, covered in plastic wrap, in the refrigerator 30 minutes.
2 Roll out the pastry between 2 sheets of plastic wrap until it is large enough to fit base and side of a 20 cm flan tin. Cut a sheet of greaseproof paper large enough to cover pastry-lined tin. Spread a layer of dried beans or rice evenly over paper. Bake 10 minutes, remove from oven and discard paper and beans. Return pastry to oven for further 5 minutes or until lightly golden. Set aside to cool.
3 To make Filling: Combine oats, caster sugar and sifted flour in large mixing bowl, make a well in the centre. Combine butter and golden syrup in a small pan. Stir over a low heat until butter has melted. Add the butter mixture to the dry ingredients. Using a wooden spoon, stir until well combined.
4 Spread pie apple into pastry shell. Spoon oat mixture on the top and smooth out with the back of a spoon. Bake for 30 minutes or until golden brown. Leave pie in tin for 15 minutes before cutting.

Cream Cheese Strudel

Preparation time:
  15 minutes
Cooking time:
  25 minutes
Serves 6

250 g cream cheese, softened
1 tablespoon lemon juice
3 tablespoons caster sugar
1/3 cup sultanas
1/4 cup plain flour
2 sheets ready-rolled puff pastry
2 tablespoons milk
1 tablespoon caster sugar, extra

1 Preheat oven to moderate 180°C. Beat the cream cheese, lemon juice and sugar together until smooth. Lightly stir in the sultanas and sifted flour.

2 Place half the cheese mixture along one side of each pastry sheet, about 5 cm in from the edge. Roll up as for a Swiss roll. Press ends together to seal.

3 Place on a greased baking sheet. Brush with milk; sprinkle with extra sugar. Bake the strudel for 25 minutes, or until golden brown.

Cream Cheese Strudel.

Apple Strudel

Preparation time:
  20 minutes
Cooking time:
  30 minutes
Serves 8

1/2 *cup ground walnuts*
1 *tablespoon soft*
  brown sugar
1 *teaspoon ground*
  cinnamon
6 *sheets filo pastry*
60 g *butter, melted*
1 x 450 g *can pie apple*
1/2 *cup sultanas*

1 Preheat oven to
moderately hot 210°C.
Combine the walnuts,
sugar and cinnamon.
Work with 1 sheet of
filo at a time, keeping
remainder covered with
a clean, damp tea-towel
to prevent drying out.
Brush first pastry sheet
with a little of the
melted butter; sprinkle
2 teaspoons of walnut
mixture over the pastry.
2 Repeat procedure
with remaining pastry
sheets, layering the
buttered sheets one on
top of the other and
sprinkling all but the
last layer with the
walnut mixture.
3 Combine the apple
and sultanas. Spread
mixture down the
centre of pastry. Fold in
the narrow ends to
meet; fold over the long
ends to make an

envelope. Place seam-
side down on a lightly
greased baking tray.
Brush the top and sides
with butter. Make
diagonal slits across the
top at 3 cm intervals.
4 Bake strudel for
15 minutes. Reduce the
heat to moderate 180°C
and cook for a further
15 minutes or until crisp
and golden. Serve warm.

Warm Strawberry and Pecan Tart

Preparation time:
  20 minutes
Cooking time:
  15 minutes
Serves 6

125 g *butter*
1/4 *cup caster sugar*
2 *eggs, lightly beaten*
1 *tablespoon golden*
  syrup
1/3 *cup/40* g *ground*
  pecans
1 *cup self-raising flour*
1 x 250 g *punnet*
  strawberries, hulled
  and sliced
1/4 *cup plum jam*
2-3 *teaspoons Grand*
  Marnier

1 Preheat oven to
moderate 180°C. Brush
a 23 cm recess flan tin
with melted butter or
oil. Coat base and side
evenly with flour; shake
off excess.
2 Using electric beaters,
beat butter and sugar in
small mixing bowl until
light and creamy. Add
eggs gradually, beating
thoroughly after each
addition. Add syrup;
beat until combined.
3 Transfer mixture to
large mixing bowl; add
pecans. Using a metal
spoon, fold in the sifted
flour. Stir until mixture
is just combined and
almost smooth.
4 Spoon the mixture
evenly into the prepared
tin; smooth surface.
Bake for 15 minutes or
until a skewer comes
out clean when inserted
in the centre.
5 Leave tart in the tin
for 8 minutes before
turning onto a wire rack.
Arrange strawberry
slices over tart base.
6 Combine the jam and
liqueur in a small pan.
Stir over low heat until
jam has melted; remove
from heat. Brush glaze
over the warm tart. Serve
at once with cream.

Note: Serve this tart
immediately to prevent
the pastry going moist.

Warm Strawberry and Pecan Tart (top),
Apple Strudel (bottom).

Crustless Chocolate Tart

Preparation time:
  20 minutes
Cooking time:
  30 minutes
Serves 6

2 cups milk
1/2 cinnamon stick,
  optional
1 teaspoon each lemon
  and orange rind, in
  thin strips
30 g butter
1/2 cup plain flour
1 tablespoon cocoa
3/4 teaspoon baking
  powder
1/2 cup caster sugar
2 eggs, separated
1/2 teaspoon imitation
  vanilla essence

Mocha Sauce
250 g chocolate, chopped
125 g butter
2/3 cup cream
1/3 cup soft brown sugar
1 tablespoon coffee
  powder

1 Place milk, cinnamon stick, rind and butter in a pan; bring to the boil. Remove from heat, cover and leave for 15 minutes. Strain milk into a bowl, discarding cinnamon and rind.
2 Combine sifted flour, cocoa and baking powder and sugar in a bowl. Combine milk, egg yolks and essence and beat gradually into flour mixture. Transfer mixture to pan. Heat, stirring constantly, until boiling. Reduce heat to a simmer, cook for 3 minutes. Remove from heat; leave to cool.
3 Preheat oven to moderate 180°C. Place egg whites in a clean, dry mixing bowl. Using electric beaters, beat until stiff peaks form. Using a metal spoon, fold into cocoa mixture. Pour into a greased 23 cm pie plate. Bake 30 minutes, or until set. Serve with Mocha Sauce.
4 To make Mocha Sauce: Place all sauce ingredients in a small pan; heat gently, stirring constantly. Serve tart cut in wedges with Mocha Sauce and cream.

Warm Date and Mascarpone Tart

Preparation time:
  25 minutes
Cooking time:
  25 minutes
Serves 6-8

4 sheets filo pastry
40 g unsalted butter,
  melted
1/4 cup ground almonds
10/220 g fresh dates,
  pitted and sliced
2 eggs
2 teaspoons custard
  powder
125 g mascarpone
  cheese
1/4 cup caster sugar
1/2 cup cream
2 tablespoons flaked
  almonds

1 Preheat oven to moderate 180°C. Brush a shallow, 10 x 35 cm fluted oblong flan tin with melted butter or oil.
2 Brush a sheet of fillo pastry sparingly with melted butter, sprinkle with ground almonds. Fold pastry sheet in half lengthways. Carefully line flan tin lengthways with pastry. Repeat process with remaining pastry, butter and nuts.
3 Spread dates evenly over the pastry base. Combine eggs, custard powder, cheese, sugar and cream in a medium bowl; whisk until smooth. Pour mixture over the dates. Sprinkle over flaked almonds. Bake for 25 minutes or until custard is golden and set. Leave tart for 10 minutes before slicing. Serve warm with whipped cream.

Note: While working, keep filo pastry covered with a damp tea-towel to prevent it drying out.

*Warm Date and Mascarpone Tart (top),
Crustless Chocolate Tart (below).*

1. *For Lemon Orange Meringue Pie: Rub butter into flour until fine and crumbly.*

2. *Roll out pastry between 2 sheets of plastic wrap to fit pie dish.*

Lemon Orange Meringue Pie

Preparation time:
  30 minutes +
  30 minutes standing
Cooking time:
  10 minutes
Serves 8

1¼ cups plain flour
1 tablespoon icing sugar
125 g butter
3 tablespoons water,
  chilled

Filling

⅓ cup plain flour
⅓ cup cornflour
⅓ cup lemon juice
⅓ cup orange juice
1 tablespoon finely
  grated lemon rind
1 tablespoon finely
  grated orange rind
1 cup caster sugar
⅔ cup water
4 egg yolks, lightly beaten
50 g butter

Topping
4 egg whites
¾ cup caster sugar

1 Preheat oven to
moderate 180°C. Sift
flour and icing sugar
into large mixing bowl;
add chopped butter.
Using fingertips, rub
butter into flour for
2 minutes or until the
mixture is a fine
crumbly texture. Add
almost all the water,
mix to form a firm
dough, adding more
liquid if necessary. Turn
onto a lightly floured
surface, knead for
1 minute or until
smooth. Store, covered
with plastic wrap, in
refrigerator for at least
30 minutes.
2 Roll out the pastry
between 2 sheets of
plastic wrap, until large
enough to cover the
base and side of a
23 cm round pie dish.

Lemon Orange Meringue Pie.

*3. Whisk over moderate heat until
mixture boils and becomes very thick.*

*4. Using electric beaters, beat egg whites
until soft peaks form.*

Cut out a sheet of greaseproof paper large enough to cover pastry-lined dish. Spread a layer of dried beans or rice evenly over paper. Bake for 10 minutes, remove from oven and discard the paper and beans. Return to oven for a further 5 minutes or until lightly golden. Set aside to cool.
3 To make Filling: Combine the sifted flours, juice, rind and sugar in a small pan, stirring until completely smooth. Add the water and stir until well combined. Whisk over moderate heat until the mixture boils and thickens. Simmer, stirring, for 2 minutes until very thick. Remove from heat and whisk in the egg yolks and butter. Allow to cool.
4 To make Topping: Place egg whites in a small, dry mixing bowl. Using electric beaters, beat the whites until soft peaks form. Add sugar gradually, beating constantly until the sugar has dissolved.
5 Pour cold filling into cold pastry shell. Spoon meringue onto filling and spread to cover. Use a flat-bladed knife to shape the meringue into peaks. Bake for 10 minutes or until the meringue is lightly browned. Serve pie warm or cold.

Quick Currant Pie

Preparation time:
  10 minutes
Cooking time:
  30 minutes
Serves 6

1½ cups/230 g currants
½ cup orange juice
2 sheets frozen puff pastry, thawed
2 tablespoons demerara sugar
30 g butter, melted
⅔ cup ground hazelnuts
1 teaspoon finely grated orange rind
1 egg, lightly beaten

1 Preheat oven to moderate 180°C. Brush a flat oven tray with melted butter. Place the currants in a large mixing bowl. Heat the orange juice and pour over currants. Allow to soak for 10 minutes, stirring occasionally.
2 Using a plate as a guide, cut a 22 cm round from one sheet of pastry and a 20 cm round from the other. Place smaller round on prepared oven tray.
3 Drain currants and return to bowl. Add sugar, butter, hazelnuts and orange rind, stir to combine. Spoon filling into the centre of the smaller pastry round, leaving a 2 cm space around the edge. Pat the filling to make a

smooth, low mound and brush the edge with beaten egg.
4 Cover with larger pastry round, and press with a fork to seal edge. Using a small, sharp knife, score the pastry lightly with curved lines coming from the centre out to the fork marks. Brush with beaten egg, bake for 30 minutes or until golden brown.

Buttermilk Nutmeg Tart

Preparation time:
  30 minutes
Cooking time:
  50 minutes
Serves 6

¾ cup plain flour
¼ cup rice flour
2 tablespoons icing sugar
100 g chilled butter, chopped
1 egg yolk, lightly beaten
1-2 teaspoons iced water

Filling
2 teaspoons custard powder
⅓ cup caster sugar
3 eggs, lightly beaten
1 teaspoon imitation vanilla essence
½ cup cream
1 cup buttermilk
1 teaspoon ground nutmeg

Buttermilk Nutmeg Tart (top), Quick Currant Pie (bottom).

1 Preheat oven to moderate 180°C. Brush a shallow, 20 cm round ovenproof pie plate with melted butter or oil.
2 Place flours and icing sugar in food processor bowl; add butter. Using the pulse action, press button for 20 seconds or until mixture is a fine, crumbly texture. Add the egg yolk and water and process for 15 seconds until the mixture comes together. Turn out onto a lightly floured surface and

knead lightly. Cover with plastic wrap and leave in the refrigerator for 10 minutes.
3 Roll pastry between 2 sheets of plastic wrap, until large enough to cover the base and sides of pie plate. Trim around pastry edge. Using fingertips, pinch a fluted pattern around the edge of the pastry.
4 To make Filling: Whisk custard powder, sugar and eggs together in a medium bowl. Add vanilla essence, cream

and buttermilk, mix until well combined. Pour mixture into the pie shell, sprinkle with nutmeg. Place tart on a baking tray. Bake for 50 minutes or until custard is set and a sharp knife comes out clean when inserted in the centre. Leave for 10 minutes before serving. Serve warm or cold with cream.

Note: Add 1 teaspoon of grated orange or lemon rind, if desired.

13

Old-fashioned Apple Pie

Preparation time:
  40 minutes
Cooking time:
  40 minutes
Serves 8

2 cups plain flour
1/4 teaspoon baking
  powder
1 tablespoon caster
  sugar
125 g butter, cut into
  pieces
1 egg, lightly beaten
3-4 tablespoons water

Filling
6 cooking apples,
  peeled, cored and
  sliced
1/2 cup caster sugar
1 tablespoon cornflour
2 teaspoons grated
  lemon rind
2 tablespoons lemon
  juice
1/2 teaspoon mixed spice
1/4 teaspoon ground
  cloves
a little milk and extra
  sugar, for glazing

1 Sift flour and baking powder in a bowl. Add the sugar. Rub in the butter with fingertips until mixture resembles fine breadcrumbs. Stir in egg and sufficient water to make a soft dough. Turn onto a lightly floured surface, knead for 1 minute or until smooth. Store, covered, in plastic wrap in the refrigerator for 15 minutes.
2 Divide dough in two, making one part a little larger than the other. Roll out the larger piece between 2 pieces of plastic wrap, until large enough to cover base and sides of a 23 cm pie plate. Prick the pastry evenly with a fork. Trim edges. Refrigerate.
3 Preheat oven to moderately hot 210°C. To make Filling: Combine apples and sugar in a large bowl. Blend cornflour with lemon rind and juice until smooth. Stir in mixed spice and cloves. Pour over apples; toss to coat. Pile apples and any liquid into pie case.
4 Roll out remaining pastry to cover the top. Brush edge of pie with milk. Place pastry over apples. Press edges to seal; trim and decorate. Brush top of pie with milk and sprinkle with extra sugar. Bake pie for 15 minutes. Reduce heat to moderate 180°C; cook for 25 minutes until pastry is golden.

Note: Roll out leftover pastry. Shape into leaves, or animals to decorate.

Pecan Pie
Preparation time:
  40 minutes
Cooking time:
  1 hour
Serves 6-8

1 1/4 cups plain flour
1/4 teaspoon baking
  powder
90 g butter, cut into
  pieces
3-4 tablespoons water

Filling
1/4 cup plain flour
1/4 cup soft brown sugar

Pecan Pie (top), Old-fashioned Apple Pie (bottom).

1 x 375 mL bottle
  maple syrup
4 eggs, lightly beaten
30 g butter, melted
1½ teaspoons imitation
  vanilla essence
1 cup pecan halves

1 Sift flour and baking powder into a bowl. Rub in the butter with fingertips until the mixture resembles fine breadcrumbs. Add 3 tablespoons water to make a firm dough, adding remaining water if necessary. Turn onto a lightly floured surface,

knead for 1 minute or until smooth. Store, covered in plastic wrap, in the refrigerator for 15 minutes.
2 Preheat oven to moderately hot 210°C. Roll out pastry between 2 pieces of plastic wrap until large enough to fit a deep, 23 cm quiche dish. Trim edges. Prick pastry evenly all over with a fork. Bake for 15 minutes or until lightly golden; remove from oven. Reduce the oven temperature to moderately slow 160°C.

3 To make Filling: Stir sifted flour and sugar together in a bowl. Using electric beaters, gradually beat in syrup, eggs, butter and vanilla essence. Stir in pecans; mix well. Pour mixture into the pastry case. Bake for 1 hour or until filling is evenly risen. Do not over-bake; the filling should be firm but still custardy. Cool on wire rack. Serve with cream or ice-cream.

Note: Pecan Pie filling will sink as it cools.

Blueberry Cheese Tart

Preparation time:
 30 minutes
Cooking time:
 45 minutes
Serves 6-8

*1 x 340 g packet pastry
 mix
125 g cream cheese
2 tablespoons caster
 sugar
1 egg, lightly beaten
1 teaspoon imitation
 vanilla essence
2 x 250 g punnets
 blueberries (see Note)
2 tablespoons seedless
 blackberry jam
2 teaspoons lemon juice
1 egg, extra, lightly
 beaten*

1 Preheat oven to
moderate 180°C. Brush
a shallow, 23 cm fluted
flan tin with melted
butter or oil.
2 Make the pastry
according to instructions
on the packet (make
either plain or sweet
pastry). Roll out pastry
between 2 sheets of
plastic wrap until large
enough to cover base
and sides of tin. Trim
edges using a sharp
knife. Re-roll remaining
pastry to a rectangle
23 x 10 cm and 2 mm
thick. Cut into long
strips 3 mm wide. Brush
with extra beaten egg.

3 Using electric beaters,
beat cream cheese and
sugar in a small mixing
bowl until light and
creamy. Add the egg
gradually, beating
thoroughly. Add the
vanilla essence; beat
until well combined.
4 Spread the cheese
mixture evenly over the
pastry; top with berries.
Combine jam and juice
in a small pan. Stir over
low heat until jam has
melted; remove from
heat. Gently spoon over
the blueberries. Lay
pastry strips in a lattice
pattern over tart; gently
press edges to base.
Trim excess pastry. Bake
45 minutes, or until
cheese mixture has set.
Leave tart in tin for 10
minutes. Serve warm or
cold with ice-cream.

Note: Substitute frozen
blueberries if desired.
Follow thawing
instructions on packet.

Bakewell Tart
Preparation time:
 15 minutes + 30
 minutes standing
Cooking time:
 35 minutes
Serves 6

*1 cup plain flour
80 g butter, chopped
2 teaspoons caster sugar
2 tablespoon water,
 chilled*

*Filling
90 g butter
1/3 cup caster sugar
2 eggs, lightly beaten
3 drops almond essence
2/3 cup ground almonds
1/3 cup self-raising flour
1 tablespoon raspberry
 jam*

*Icing
2 tablespoons icing
 sugar
1/2 teaspoon lemon juice
1/2 teaspoon hot water*

1 Preheat oven to
moderate 180°C. Sift
flour into large mixing
bowl; add chopped
butter. Using fingertips,
rub butter into flour for
2 minutes or until
mixture is a fine,
crumbly texture; stir in
sugar. Add almost all
the liquid, mix to a firm
dough, adding more
liquid if necessary. Turn
onto a lightly floured
surface, knead 1 minute
or until smooth. Store,
covered with plastic
wrap, in refrigerator for
30 minutes.
2 Roll out the pastry
between 2 sheets of
plastic wrap, large
enough to cover base
and side of a 20 cm flan
tin. Cut out a sheet of
greaseproof paper large
enough to cover pastry-
lined tin. Spread a layer
of dried beans or rice
evenly over paper. Bake
10 minutes, remove
from oven and discard

Blueberry Cheese Tart (top), Bakewell Tart (bottom).

paper and beans.
Return pastry to oven
for further 5 minutes or
until lightly golden. Set
aside to cool.
3 To make Filling:
Using electric beaters,
beat butter and sugar in
a small mixing bowl
until light and creamy.
Add the eggs gradually,
beating thoroughly
after each addition.

Add essence; beat until
combined. Transfer
mixture to large mixing
bowl. Using a metal
spoon, fold in ground
almonds and sifted flour.
4 Spread raspberry jam
over base of the pastry
shell. Spoon almond
mixture on top and
smooth surface. Bake
for 35 minutes or until
golden brown.

5 To make Icing: Place
sifted icing sugar in a
small jug. Stir in lemon
juice and just enough
water to make a smooth
mixture. Drizzle in an
abstract pattern over
cold tart to decorate.

Note: To serve as a
dessert, omit the icing
and serve tart warm
with custard or cream.

17

1. For Deep Dish Apple Pie: Simmer apples for 10 minutes until just tender.

2. Process flours, butter and sugar until mixture is a fine, crumbly texture.

Deep Dish Apple Pie

Preparation time:
 1 hour
Cooking time:
 50 minutes
Serves 6-8

1 cup self-raising flour
1 cup plain flour
125 g chilled butter,
  chopped
2 tablespoons caster
  sugar
1 egg
1-2 tablespoons milk
1 egg, extra, lightly
  beaten

Filling
8 large green apples,
  peeled, cut into
  12 wedges
2 thick strips lemon rind
6 whole cloves
1 cinnamon stick
2 cups water
1/2 cup sugar

1 Preheat oven to moderate 180°C. Brush a deep, 20 cm round springform tin with melted butter or oil. Line base with paper; grease paper. Dust tin lightly with flour, shake off excess.

2 To make Filling: Combine apples, rind, cloves, cinnamon, water and sugar in a large pan. Cover and simmer 10 minutes or until only just tender; remove from heat; drain well. Discard rind, cloves and cinnamon. Set aside.

3 Place flours and butter in a food processor bowl; add sugar. Using the pulse action, press button for 15 seconds or until the mixture is a fine crumbly texture. Add egg and almost all the milk; process a further 15 seconds until the mixture comes together,

adding more liquid if necessary. Turn onto a lightly floured surface, knead for 2 minutes or until smooth. Store, covered in plastic wrap, in the refrigerator for 15 minutes.

4 Roll two-thirds of the pastry between 2 sheets of plastic wrap until large enough to cover base and side of tin. Carefully spoon apple into pie shell. Roll remaining pastry into a circle large enough to cover the top of the pie. Brush pastry edges with a little of the extra beaten egg to seal. Trim edges with a sharp knife and press around edge with a fork. Brush top with beaten egg. Bake for 50 minutes or until pastry is golden and cooked through. Leave the pie in the tin for 10 minutes before removing. Serve hot or cold with cream, ice-cream or custard.

Deep Dish Apple Pie.

3. Roll remaining pastry into a circle large enough to cover the top of the pie.

4. Brush edges with beaten egg to seal. Trim with a sharp knife.

Treacle Macadamia Tart

Preparation time:
  45 minutes
Cooking time:
  1 hour
Serves 8

1¾ cups plain flour
150 g chilled butter,
  chopped
2-3 tablespoons iced
  water

Filling
1 tablespoon
  self-raising flour
¼ teaspoon ground
  ginger
½ cup soft brown sugar
2 eggs, lightly beaten
25 g butter, melted
⅓ cup treacle
1 teaspoon finely grated
  lemon rind
2 tablespoons sour
  cream
100 g macadamia nuts,
  roughly chopped

1 Preheat oven to
moderate 180°C. Brush
a shallow, 23 cm fluted
flan tin with melted
butter or oil.
2 Place the flour and
butter in food processor
bowl. Using the pulse
action, press button for
20 seconds or until the
mixture is a fine
crumbly texture.
3 Add almost all the
liquid and process for
15 seconds, until the

mixture comes together,
adding more liquid if
necessary. Store pastry,
covered with plastic
wrap, in the refrigerator
for 10 minutes.
4 Turn dough onto
lightly floured surface;
knead 2 minutes or
until smooth. Roll
pastry between 2 sheets
of plastic wrap, large
enough to cover base
and sides of flan tin.
Press pastry into tin and
trim edges with sharp
knife. Cut a sheet of
greaseproof paper large
enough to cover
pastry-lined tin. Spread
a layer of dried beans
or rice evenly over the
paper. Bake for
20 minutes. Remove
from oven; discard
paper and beans.
Return pastry to oven
for a further 10 minutes.
5 To make Filling:
Place flour, ginger,
sugar and eggs in a
medium bowl. Stir until
well combined. Add
remaining ingredients,
mix well. Pour mixture
into baked pastry shell.
Bake for 25 minutes, or
until filling is set.
6 Leave tart in tin for
10 minutes before
removing. Serve warm
or cold with cream.

Country-style Blackberry Pie

Preparation time:
  45 minutes
Cooking time:
  45 minutes
Serves 6-8

2 cups self-raising flour
2 tablespoons icing
  sugar
2 tablespoons custard
  powder
250 g chilled butter,
  chopped
1 egg, lightly beaten
¼ cup water
1 tablespoon raw sugar
1 egg, extra, lightly
  beaten

Filling
¼ cup cornflour
2 x 425 g cans
  blackberries, drained,
  juice reserved
2 tablespoons caster
  sugar
1 teaspoon finely grated
  orange rind

1 Preheat oven to
moderate 180°C. Brush a
shallow, 23 cm round
ovenproof pie plate with
melted butter or oil.
2 To make Filling:
Blend cornflour with a
small amount of the
reserved blackberry
juice in a small bowl
until smooth. Combine
the remaining juice,
sugar, orange rind and
cornflour mixture in a

Country-style Blackberry Pie (top), Treacle Macadamia Tart (bottom).

medium pan. Stir over low heat 5 minutes, or until mixture boils and thickens. Remove from heat; set aside to cool.
3 Place the flour, icing sugar, custard powder and butter in food processor bowl. Using the pulse action, press button 15 seconds or until mixture is a fine, crumbly texture. Add egg and water, process 15 seconds until the mixture comes together, adding more liquid if necessary. Turn onto a well-floured surface, knead 2 minutes or until smooth. Store, covered with plastic wrap, in the refrigerator 15 minutes.
4 Roll two-thirds of pastry on a well-floured surface until large enough to cover base and sides of pie plate. Spread cornflour mixture evenly into pie shell, top with blackberries. Roll remaining pastry into a circle large enough to cover top of the pie. Brush edges with extra egg to seal. Trim edges with a sharp knife. Brush the top of the pie with egg. Using a fork, make a pattern around edge. Sprinkle with sugar. Bake for 35 minutes or until the pastry is crisp and golden. Let pie stand for 5 minutes before serving. Serve hot with cream or ice-cream.

Steamed puddings

Thinking comfort food? Think steamed puddings. For warming up chilly winter evenings, there is nothing quite like a beautifully turned out, hot steamed pudding with custard. In summer, serve individual puddings with ice-cream and fruit. The evergreen traditional Christmas pudding is still the mightiest of them all, but any of these recipes makes a great, nostaligic treat all year round.

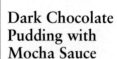

Dark Chocolate Pudding with Mocha Sauce

Preparation time:
  30 minutes
Cooking time:
  1 hour 25 minutes
Serves 6

1¼ cups self-raising
  flour
1 cup plain flour
¼ cup cocoa powder
¼ teaspoon
  bicarbonate of soda
150 g butter
½ cup caster sugar
¼ cup soft dark brown
  sugar
100 g dark chocolate,
  chopped
1 teaspoon imitation
  vanilla essence
2 eggs, lightly beaten
¾ cup buttermilk

Mocha Sauce
50 g butter
150 g dark chocolate,
  chopped
1½ cups cream
1 tablespoon instant
  coffee powder
1-2 tablespoons
  chocolate liqueur

1 Brush an 8-cup capacity pudding basin or steamer with melted butter or oil. Line base with paper, grease paper. Grease a large sheet of aluminium foil and a large sheet of greaseproof paper. Lay the paper over the foil, greased side up. Pleat it in the centre. Set aside.
2 Sift flours, cocoa and soda into a large mixing bowl. Make a well in the centre. Combine butter, sugars, chocolate and essence in a pan.

Dark Chocolate Pudding with Mocha Sauce.

Stir over low heat until butter and chocolate have melted and sugars have dissolved; remove from heat. Add the butter mixture, beaten eggs and buttermilk to dry ingredients. Using a wooden spoon, stir until well combined; do not overbeat.

3 Spoon mixture into prepared basin. Cover with the greased foil and paper, greased side down. Place lid over foil and secure clips. If you have no lid, lay a pleated tea-towel over foil, tie it securely with string under the lip of the basin. Knot the four ends of the tea-towel together; this acts as a handle to help lower the basin into the pan.

4 Place the basin on a trivet in a large, deep pan. Carefully pour boiling water down the side of the pan to come half-way up the side of the basin. Bring to the boil; cover and cook for 1 hour 15 minutes. Do not let the pudding boil dry; replenish with boiling water as the pudding is cooking. When cooked, remove covering, invert onto a plate. Serve hot with Mocha Sauce.

5 To make Mocha Sauce: Combine butter, chocolate, cream and coffee powder. Stir over low heat until the butter

and chocolate have melted and the mixture is smooth. Add the chocolate liqueur, stir until well combined; remove from heat.

Note: The pudding and sauce can be reheated in a microwave oven. Store pudding, covered, in the refrigerator until ready to use.

Fruit Mince Pudding with Citrus Sauce
Preparation time:
  15 minutes
Cooking time:
  1 hour 30 minutes
Serves 6

125 g butter
3/4 cup caster sugar
2 eggs, lightly beaten
2 teaspoons finely
  grated orange rind
1/2 cup fruit mince
1 1/2 cups self-raising
  flour
1/4 cup milk
1/4 cup orange juice

Citrus Sauce
1 cup orange juice
1/2 cup lemon juice
1 tablespoon finely
  grated orange rind
2 teaspoons finely
  grated lemon rind
1 cup water
1 tablespoon cornflour
1 teaspoon butter
1 egg yolk

1 Brush an 18 cm, 6-cup capacity pudding basin or steamer with melted butter or oil. Line base with paper, grease paper. Grease a large sheet of aluminium foil and a large sheet of greaseproof paper. Lay the paper over the foil, greased side up, pleat it in the centre. Set aside.

2 Using electric beaters, beat butter and sugar in small mixing bowl until light and creamy. Add eggs gradually, beating thoroughly after each addition. Stir in rind.

3 Transfer mixture to large mixing bowl; add fruit mince. Using a metal spoon, fold in sifted flour alternately with liquids. Stir until mixture is just combined and almost smooth.

4 Spoon mixture into prepared basin. Cover with the greased foil and paper, greased side down. Place lid over foil and secure clips. If you have no lid, lay a pleated tea-towel over foil, tie it securely with string under the lip of the basin. Knot the four ends of the tea-towel together, this acts as a handle to help lower the basin in to the pan.

5 Place the basin on a trivet in a large, deep pan. Carefully pour boiling water down the side of the pan to come half-way up the side of

Fruit Mince Pudding with Citrus Sauce.

the basin. Bring to the boil, cover, cook for 1 hour 30 minutes. Do not let the pudding boil dry; replenish with boiling water as the pudding cooks. Once cooked, leave pudding in tin for 5 minutes before uncovering and inverting onto a plate. Serve warm with Citrus Sauce passed separately.
6 To make Citrus Sauce: Place orange and lemon juice and rinds in a small pan. Combine the cornflour with a little water to make a smooth paste; add remaining water to pan and bring to boil. Add cornflour paste; stir until sauce thickens and clears. Stir in butter. Remove pan from heat, cool slightly, then beat in egg yolk. Strain through a fine sieve into a serving jug.

25

Golden Syrup Pumpkin Pudding with Custard Sauce

Preparation time:
35 minutes
Cooking time:
1 hour 45 minutes
Serves 6-8

2 cups self-raising flour
1/2 teaspoon ground mixed spice
125 g butter

1/2 cup soft brown sugar
1/4 cup golden syrup
2 eggs, lightly beaten
1/4 cup milk
1/2 cup cooked mashed pumpkin, cooled

Custard Sauce
1 tablespoon custard powder
2 tablespoons caster sugar
2 tablespoons golden syrup
1/2 cup milk
1 cup cream

1 Brush an 8-cup capacity pudding basin or steamer with melted butter or oil. Line base with paper, grease the paper. Grease a large sheet of aluminium foil and a large sheet of greaseproof paper. Lay the paper over the foil, greased side up. Pleat it in the centre. Set aside.
2 Sift flour and mixed spice into a large mixing bowl. Combine butter, sugar and syrup

From left: Lemon Pudding, Golden Syrup Pumpkin Pudding with Custard Sauce.

in a small pan. Stir over low heat until butter has melted and sugar dissolved; remove from heat. Add the butter mixture, eggs and milk to dry ingredients. Using a wooden spoon, stir until mixture is well combined. Stir in the cooled pumpkin; do not overbeat.

3 Spoon mixture into prepared basin. Cover with the greased foil and paper, greased side down. Place lid over foil and secure clips. If you have no lid, lay a pleated tea-towel over foil, tie it securely with string under the lip of the basin. Knot the four ends of the tea-towel together; this acts as a handle to help you lower the basin into the pan.

4 Place the basin on a trivet in a large, deep pan. Carefully pour boiling water down the side of the pan to come half-way up the side of the basin. Bring to the boil; cover, cook for 1 hour 45 minutes. Do not let the pudding boil dry; replenish with boiling water as the pudding cooks. Serve immediately with warm Custard Sauce.

5 To make Custard Sauce: Combine the custard powder, sugar, syrup and milk in a small bowl; stir until smooth. Transfer

mixture to a medium pan, add cream, stir over medium heat for 5 minutes or until the sauce boils and thickens; remove from heat, pour over pudding.

Lemon Pudding
Preparation time:
  20 minutes
Cooking time:
  1 hour
Serves 4-6

90 g butter
1/3 cup caster sugar
2 eggs, lightly beaten
1 teaspoon imitation
  vanilla essence
2 teaspoons finely
  grated lemon rind
1 cup self-raising flour
1/4 cup milk

1 Brush a 4-cup capacity pudding basin or steamer with melted butter or oil. Line base with paper, grease the paper. Grease a large sheet of aluminium foil and a large sheet of greaseproof paper. Lay the paper over the foil, greased side up, pleat it in the centre. Set aside.
2 Using electric beaters, beat butter and sugar in a

small mixing bowl until light and fluffy. Add eggs one at a time, beating well after each addition. Add essence and orange rind; beat until combined.
3 Transfer mixture to large mixing bowl. Using a metal spoon, fold in sifted flour alternately with milk; stir until just combined and the mixture is almost smooth.
4 Spoon mixture into prepared basin. Cover with the greased foil and paper, greased side down. Place lid over foil, and secure clips. If you have no lid, lay a pleated tea-towel over foil, tie it securely with string under the lip of the basin. Knot the four ends of the tea-towel together; this acts as a handle to help you lower the basin into the pan.
5 Place the basin on a trivet in a large, deep pan. Carefully pour boiling water down the side of the pan to come half-way up the side of the basin. Bring to the boil, cover, and cook for 1 hour. Do not let the pudding boil dry, replenish with boiling water as the pudding cooks. Remove the lid and covering and invert pudding onto a plate. Serve warm or cold with cream, custard or vanilla ice-cream.

1. *For Classic Christmas Pudding: Line base with paper, grease paper.*

2. *Carefully skim membrane from the suet and discard. Chop suet finely.*

Classic Christmas Pudding

Preparation time:
  20 minutes
Cooking time:
  7 hours
Serves 12-16

375 g fresh suet
6 cups/360 g fine fresh
  breadcrumbs
4½ cups/720 g raisins
1⅔ cups/250 g currants
1½ cups/235 g chopped
  mixed peel
8 eggs, lightly beaten
⅔ cup brandy
extra brandy, for
  flaming pudding

1 Brush a 7-cup capacity pudding basin or steamer with melted butter or oil. Line base with paper, grease the paper. Grease a large sheet of aluminium foil and a large sheet of greaseproof paper. Lay the paper over the foil, greased side up, pleat it in the centre. Set aside.
2 Carefully skim the membrane from suet and discard. Chop suet finely either by hand or in a food processor. Transfer to a very large mixing bowl. Add the breadcrumbs, raisins, currants and mixed peel; mix until they are thoroughly combined.
3 Add eggs to fruit mixture and mix well. Gradually add brandy, combining thoroughly. Stir well.
4 Spoon mixture into prepared basin. Cover with the greased foil and paper, greased side down. Place lid over foil and secure clips. If you have no lid, lay a pleated tea-towel over foil, tie it securely with string under the lip of the basin. Knot the four ends of the tea-towel together; this acts as a handle to help you lower the basin in to the cooking pan.
5 Place the basin on a trivet in a large, deep pan. Carefully pour boiling water down the side of the pan to come half-way up the side of the basin. Bring to the boil, cover, and cook for 7 hours. Do not let pudding boil dry; replenish with boiling water as the pudding cooks. Remove from pan; cool and re-cover. Store up to 3 months in a cool, dry place (keep refrigerated in hot, humid weather).
6 To serve: Steam again as directed above for 2 hours. Unmould onto a shallow, flameproof serving dish. Heat a little extra brandy, pour around pudding and ignite. Serve with the sauce of your choice or brandy butter.

Classic Christmas Pudding.

3. Add the beaten eggs to combined fruit and breadcrumbs and mix well.

4. Place lid of steamer over the foil, and secure clips.

29

Raisin Pudding

Preparation time:
  30 minutes
Cooking time:
  1 hour
Serves 4-6

125 g butter
1/2 cup caster sugar
2 eggs, separated
2 teaspoon finely grated
  lemon rind
1 cup self-raising flour
2 tablespoons lemon
  juice
3/4 cup raisins

1 Brush a 4-cup capacity pudding basin or steamer with melted butter or oil. Line base with paper, grease paper. Grease a large sheet of aluminium foil and a large sheet of greaseproof paper. Lay the paper over the foil, greased side up, pleat it in the centre. Set aside.
2 Using electric beaters, beat butter and sugar in small mixing bowl until light and fluffy. Add egg yolks one at a time, beating well after each addition. Add rind; beat until combined.
3 Transfer mixture to large mixing bowl. Using a metal spoon, fold in the sifted flour, lemon juice and raisins. Stir until just combined and the mixture is almost smooth. Using electric beaters, beat egg whites

in a small, clean, dry mixing bowl until stiff peaks form. Using a metal spoon, fold egg whites lightly into the batter mixture.
4 Spoon mixture into prepared basin. Cover with the greased foil and paper, greased side down. Place lid over foil and secure clips. If you have no lid, lay a pleated tea-towel over foil, tie it securely with string under the lip of the basin. Knot the four ends of the tea-towel together; this acts as a handle to help you lower the basin into the pan.
5 Place the basin on a trivet in a large, deep pan. Carefully pour boiling water down the side of the pan to come half-way up the side of the basin.
6 Bring to the boil, cover, cook for 1 hour. Do not let pudding boil dry, replenish with boiling water as the pudding cooks. Remove covering, invert onto a plate. Serve warm, with the sauce of your choice.

Orange and Ginger Pudding

Preparation time:
  30 minutes
Cooking time:
  1 hour 15 minutes
Serves 4-6

125 g butter
1/2 cup caster sugar
2 eggs, separated
2 teaspoons grated
  orange rind
1 cup self-raising flour
2 tablespoons orange
  juice
2 tablespoons chopped
  preserved ginger,
  optional

1 Brush a 4-cup capacity pudding basin or steamer with melted butter or oil. Line base with paper, grease paper. Grease a large sheet of aluminium foil and a large sheet of greaseproof paper. Lay the paper over the foil, greased side up, pleat it in the centre. Set aside.
2 Using electric beaters, beat butter and sugar in small mixing bowl until light and fluffy. Add egg yolks one at a time, beating well after each addition. Add rind; beat until combined.
3 Transfer mixture to a large mixing bowl. Using a metal spoon, fold in the sifted flour, orange juice and ginger,

Orange and Ginger Pudding (top), Raisin Pudding (bottom).

if using. Stir until just combined and mixture is almost smooth. Using electric beaters, beat egg whites in a small, dry mixing bowl until stiff peaks form. Using a metal spoon, fold lightly into batter mixture.

4 Spoon mixture into prepared basin. Cover with the greased foil and paper, greased side down. Place lid over foil and secure clips. If you have no lid, lay a pleated tea-towel over foil, tie it securely with string under the lip of the basin. Knot the four ends of the tea-towel together; this acts as a handle to help you lower the basin into the pan.

5 Place the basin on a trivet in a large, deep pan. Carefully pour boiling water down the side of the pan to come half-way up the side of the basin.

6 Bring to the boil, cover and cook for 1 hour 15 minutes. Do not let pudding boil dry, replenish with boiling water as it cooks. Remove covering, invert onto a plate. Serve with custard, garnished with grated orange rind or ginger, if liked.

31

Ginger Marmalade Pudding

Preparation time:
15 minutes
Cooking time:
1 hour 30 minutes
Serves 6

90 g butter
1/2 cup caster sugar
2 eggs, lightly beaten
2 tablespoons ginger
 marmalade
1 1/2 cups self-raising
 flour
1 teaspoon ground
 ginger
1/3 cup buttermilk

Syrup
1/3 cup ginger
 marmalade
1 tablespoon soft
 brown sugar
1 tablespoon caster
 sugar
1 cup water

1 Brush an 18 cm, 6-cup capacity pudding basin or steamer with melted butter or oil. Line base with paper, grease paper. Grease a large sheet of aluminium foil and a large sheet of greaseproof paper. Lay the paper over the foil, greased side up, pleat it in the centre. Set aside.
2 Using electric beaters, beat butter and sugar in small mixing bowl until light and creamy. Add

eggs gradually, beating thoroughly after each addition. Add the ginger marmalade; beat until combined.
3 Transfer mixture to a large mixing bowl. Using a metal spoon, fold in the sifted dry ingredients alternately with the buttermilk. Stir until just combined and almost smooth.
4 Spoon mixture into prepared basin. Cover with the greased foil and paper, greased side down. Place lid over foil and secure clips. If you have no lid, lay a pleated tea-towel over foil, tie it securely with string under the lip of the basin. Knot the four ends of the tea-towel together; this acts as a handle to help lower the basin into the pan.
5 Place the basin on a trivet in a large, deep pan. Carefully pour boiling water down the side of the pan to come half-way up the side of the basin. Bring to the boil, cover, cook for 1 hour 30 minutes. Do not let the pudding boil dry, replenish with boiling water as it cooks. Remove covering from pudding and invert onto a plate; pour the Syrup over the pudding while it is hot. Serve warm with cream or custard.
6 To make Syrup: Combine all ingredients

in a small pan. Stir over low heat until the mixture boils and sugar has dissoved. Simmer, uncovered, without stirring for 10 minutes.

Note: For extra flavour, add 1 tablespoon of whisky, brandy or liqueur to the custard.

Sago Plum Puddings with Custard

Preparation time:
30 minutes +
 overnight soaking
Cooking time:
1 hour 10 minutes
Serves 4

1/3 cup sago
1 cup milk
1/3 cup caster sugar
25 g butter, melted
1 tablespoon honey
1 teaspoon finely grated
 orange rind
1 cup/60 g fine fresh
 white breadcrumbs
3/4 cup currants
thin strips orange rind,
 for garnish, optional

Custard
2 teaspoons custard
 powder
2 tablespoons caster
 sugar
1 cup milk
1 teaspoon imitation
 vanilla essence
2 egg yolks, lightly
 beaten

1 Soak sago overnight in water to cover. Brush 4 x ½ cup capacity heatproof moulds with oil. Grease 4 small sheets of aluminium foil and 4 small sheets of greaseproof paper. Lay the paper over the foil, greased side up.

2 Drain sago. Combine sago and milk with the remaining ingredients in a medium bowl. Spoon mixture evenly into the moulds. Cover each with the greased foil and paper, greased side down. Tie with string.

3 Place the moulds in a deep pan on a flat trivet. Carefully pour boiling water down the side of the pan to come half-way up the sides of the moulds. Bring to the boil, cover, cook for 1 hour. Do not let the puddings boil dry; replenish with boiling water as the puddings cook. Remove puddings with tongs. Turn out and serve with warm Custard. Garnish with orange rind, if desired.

4 To make Custard: Blend custard powder and sugar in a small bowl with a small amount of milk until smooth. Pour in the remaining milk, stir. Transfer the mixture to a small pan, stir over medium heat until the custard boils and thickens. Remove from heat. Whisk in essence and egg yolks. Strain through a fine sieve.

Ginger Marmalade Pudding (top), Sago Plum Pudding with Custard (bottom).

Steamed Fig Pudding with Quick Brandy Custard

Preparation time:
 15 minutes
Cooking time:
 1 hour 30 minutes
Serves 8

1½ cups self-raising
 flour
¾ cup plain flour
2 teaspoons mixed spice
½ teaspoon
 bicarbonate of soda
¼ cup powdered milk
150 g butter
¾ cup soft brown sugar
1 cup/210 g dried figs,
 chopped
¾ cup water
2 eggs, lightly beaten

Quick Brandy Custard
2½ cups prepared
 custard
1¼ cups cream
¼ cup brandy

1 Brush a 21 cm, 8-cup capacity pudding basin or steamer with melted butter or oil. Line base with paper, grease paper. Grease a large sheet of aluminium foil and a large sheet of greaseproof paper. Lay the paper over the foil, greased side up, pleat it in the centre. Set aside.
2 Sift the flours with the remaining dry ingredients into a large mixing bowl. Make a well in the centre. Combine butter, sugar, figs and water in a small pan. Stir over low heat until butter has melted and sugar has dissolved.
3 Add butter mixture and beaten eggs to dry ingredients. Stir until just combined; do not overbeat mixture.
4 Spoon mixture into prepared basin. Cover with the greased foil and paper, greased side

down. Place lid over foil and secure clips. If you have no lid, lay a pleated tea-towel over foil, tie it securely with string under the lip of the basin. Knot the four ends of the tea-towel together; this acts as a handle to help you lower the basin into the pan.
5 Place the basin on a trivet in a large, deep pan. Carefully pour boiling water down the side of the pan to come halfway up the side of the basin. Bring to the boil, cover, cook for 1 hour 30 minutes. Do not let the pudding boil dry. Remove covering, invert onto a plate. Serve warm with Quick Brandy Custard.
6 To make Quick Brandy Custard: Place all ingredients in a small pan. Stir over low heat until warmed through. Do not let mixture boil.

Steamed Fig Pudding with Quick Brandy Custard.

1. *For Steamed Fig Pudding: Lay paper over the foil, greased side up and pleat.*

2. *Stir over low heat until butter has melted and sugar has dissolved.*

3. Secure tea-towel with string. Knot the four ends together to form a handle.

4. Carefully pour boiling water down the side to come halfway up the basin.

Baked puddings

S ometimes the simple, familiar pleasures are the best. Among our recipes are classics such as Apple Charlotte and Baked Egg Custard – dishes that are sure to evoke happy childhood memories of your grandmother's cooking. Other firm favourites have been updated; we've given Lemon Delicious a hint of lime and these luscious (yet easy to make) self-saucing puddings will make a graceful end to any mealtime gathering.

❖   ❖   ❖   ❖

Pineapple Upside-down Pudding

Preparation time:
  15 minutes
Cooking time:
  45 minutes
Makes 1 x 20 cm round cake

10 g butter, melted
1 tablespoon desiccated
  coconut
¼ cup soft brown sugar
1 x 440 g can sliced
  pineapple, drained
90 g butter
½ cup caster sugar
2 eggs, lightly beaten
1 teaspoon vanilla
  essence
1 cup self-raising flour
⅓ cup coconut milk

1 Preheat oven to moderate 180°C. Brush base and sides of a 20 cm ring tin with melted butter or oil. Sprinkle coconut and sugar over base, cut pineapple slices in half. Arrange over coconut.
2 Using electric beaters, beat butter and sugar in a small mixing bowl until light and creamy. Add eggs gradually, beating thoroughly after each addition. Add vanilla essence; beat until combined.
3 Transfer the mixture to a large mixing bowl. Using a metal spoon, fold in the sifted flour alternately with the coconut milk. Stir until mixture is just combined and almost smooth.

Pineapple Upside-down Cake (top), Butterscotch Self-saucing Puddings (below).

4 Carefully spoon mixture into prepared tin; smooth surface. Bake 45 minutes or until skewer comes out clean when inserted in centre of cake. Leave cake in tin 5 minutes before turning onto a serving plate. Serve with custard or cream.

Note: This pudding is delicious served cold as a cake with cream.

Butterscotch Self-saucing Puddings

Preparation time:
  15 minutes
Cooking time:
  35 minutes
Serves 6

90 g butter, chopped
1 cup soft brown
  sugar
1½ cups self-raising
  flour
1 teaspoon mixed
  spice
¾ cup milk
60 g butter, extra
½ cup sugar
¼ cup water
1 cup water, extra

1 Preheat oven to moderate 180°C. Brush 6 x 1-cup capacity ovenproof dishes with melted butter or oil.

2 Using electric beaters, beat butter and sugar in small mixing bowl until light and creamy. Transfer mixture to a large mixing bowl. Using a metal spoon, fold sifted flour and mixed spice into butter mixture alternately with milk. Spoon mixture evenly into prepared dishes. Place on a baking tray; set aside.
3 Place extra butter, sugar and ¼ cup water in a small pan. Stir over low heat until butter has melted and sugar has dissolved. Bring to the boil. Reduce heat and simmer gently, uncovered, until golden brown. Remove from heat. Very carefully stir in extra water. Stir over a low heat until smooth; cool slightly.
4 Pour an equal amount of the mixture over each pudding. Bake for 35 minutes, or until a skewer comes out clean when inserted in the centre. Loosen edges of each pudding by running a knife around the edge. Invert onto serving plate.

Note: To make one big pudding, pour mixture in a greased 4-cup capacity dish, top with melted sugar mixture. Bake at 180°C for 35-40 minutes.

Meringue Rice Pudding.

Meringue Rice Pudding

Preparation time:
  30 minutes
Cooking time:
  10 minutes
Serves 4

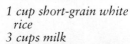

1 cup short-grain white
  rice
3 cups milk

3 tablespoons caster
   sugar
2 eggs, *separated*
1/3 cup apricot jam,
   warmed
1 tablespoon caster
   sugar, *extra*

1 Preheat oven to moderate 180°C. Combine rice, milk and sugar in a pan. Bring to the boil, cover, reduce heat to low.

2 Simmer rice gently for 12 minutes or until rice is tender and most of the milk has been absorbed. Remove from heat; leave, covered, until all the milk has been absorbed (this will take about 10 minutes). Stir in the egg yolks.

3 Spread jam over the base of a greased 6-cup capacity ovenproof dish. Pour the cooked rice mixture over.

4 Place egg whites in a small, clean, dry mixing bowl. Using electric beaters, beat until stiff peaks form. Add extra caster sugar gradually, beating constantly until dissolved and the mixture is glossy and thick. Spread over rice. Bake for 10 minutes or until meringue has set and browned slightly.

Black Forest Self-saucing Pudding

Preparation time:
 20 minutes
Cooking time:
 25 minutes
Serves 4

*1 x 425 g can pitted
 dark cherries, drained
1 x 225 g packet instant
 chocolate self-saucing
 pudding*

1 Preheat oven to moderate 180°C. Brush a deep, 20 cm round ovenproof dish with melted butter or oil.
2 Place the cherries in the base of the dish. Prepare chocolate pudding according to instructions on the packet. Decrease the amount of water in the sauce to ½ cup. Pour the pudding mixture over the dark cherries; smooth surface.
3 Top with sauce mix. Bake 25 minutes, or until skewer comes out clean when inserted in the centre of pudding. Serve immediately.

Baked Peach Pudding

Preparation time:
 30 minutes
Cooking time:
 35 minutes
Serves 6

*2 cups self-raising flour
125 g butter
½ cup caster sugar
100 g marzipan
2 tablespoons citrus jam
2 tablespoons peach
 schnapps or orange
 juice
150 g dried peaches,
 chopped
½ cup peach nectar
2 eggs, lightly beaten*

Peach Sauce
*1 x 440 g can peach
 halves, with juice
1-2 tablespoons peach
 schnapps (optional)*

1 Preheat oven to moderate 180°C. Brush a deep, 20 cm (6-cup capacity) baba tin with melted butter or oil.
2 Sift flour into a large mixing bowl. Combine butter, sugar, marzipan, jam, schnapps, dried peaches and nectar in a medium pan. Stir over low heat until butter and marzipan have melted and sugar has dissolved; remove from heat.

3 Add butter mixture and eggs to flour. Using a wooden spoon, stir until well combined; do not overbeat. Spoon mixture evenly into prepared tin; smooth the surface. Bake for 35 minutes, or until a skewer comes out clean when inserted in centre of pudding. Leave the pudding in the tin for 10 minutes before turning out. Serve warm with Peach Sauce.
4 To make Peach Sauce: Place the peaches and juice and the schnapps, if using, in a food processor or blender bowl. Using the pulse action, press button for 20 seconds, or until mixture is smooth. Transfer to a small pan. Stir over low heat for 2 minutes or until the sauce is warmed through.

Note: This pudding recipe is very adaptable. Other dried fruits can be substituted for the peaches, and canned fruit, such as dark pitted cherries, apricots or pears can be used in the sauce. It can also be served cold with rich vanilla, cinnamon or peach ice-cream. Serve on the same day it is cooked for best results.

*Baked Peach Pudding (top), Black Forest
Self-saucing Pudding (bottom).*

40

1. *For Individual Apple Charlottes: Cut rounds from the bread slices.*

2. *Press bread fingers around the sides of each dish, overlapping slightly.*

Individual Apple Charlottes with Jam Sauce

Preparation time:
  30 minutes
Cooking time:
  20 minutes
Serves 6

*5 cooking apples,
  peeled, cored
2 tablespoons soft
  brown sugar
1/4 teaspoon ground
  cinnamon
1 loaf day-old white
  bread, crusts removed
100 g butter, melted*

*Jam Sauce
1 cup strawberry jam
1 cup water
1 teaspoon grated
  lemon rind
1/2 cup caster sugar*

1 Preheat oven to moderate 180°C. Brush 6 x 1-cup capacity ovenproof dishes with melted butter or oil. Slice apple thinly and place in a saucepan with sugar, cinnamon and enough water to cover. Cook until tender and drain well; cool.
2 Using a biscuit cutter, cut rounds from bread slices to fit tops and bases of each dish. Cut remaining slices into fingers 2 cm wide, trim to fit height of dish. Dip first round into melted butter and place in base of dish. Dip each finger of bread into melted butter and press around sides of dish vertically, overlapping them slightly. Line all the dishes with bread in this manner (see Note).

3 Fill each bread-lined dish evenly with cooked apple, and top with last round of bread, which has been dipped in melted butter. Press down gently to seal. Place dishes on baking tray and bake for 20 minutes. Turn out on to individual plates. Serve warm with Jam Sauce and cream.
4 To make Jam Sauce: Place all the sauce ingredients in a small pan, bring to boil and simmer for 15 minutes. Strain and serve hot.

Note: You may not need the whole loaf of bread; adjust the amount to fit your dishes.

HINT
For good results when beating egg whites for meringue: always use a completely clean and dry bowl, just a trace of oil will stop whites whipping; and make sure all sugar crystals have dissolved.

Individual Apple Charlotte with Jam Sauce.

3. *Top with a round of bread dipped in butter. Press down gently to seal.*

4. *Simmer sauce for 15 minutes, strain into a serving jug and serve hot.*

Classic Baked Egg Custard

Preparation time:
  5 minutes
Cooking time:
  30 minutes
Serves 4-6

3 eggs, lightly beaten
1/3 cup caster sugar
2 cups milk
1 teaspoon imitation
  vanilla essence
1/4 teaspoon ground
  nutmeg

1 Preheat oven to moderate 180°C. Brush a deep 4-cup capacity ovenproof dish with melted butter or oil.
2 Whisk eggs, sugar, milk and essence in a medium mixing bowl for 2 minutes. Strain into prepared dish; sprinke with nutmeg.
3 Place dish into a shallow baking dish. Pour in enough hot water to come halfway up the sides. Bake for 30 minutes or until custard is set and a knife comes out clean when inserted in the centre. Remove dish from waterbath immediately.

Note: Add 1/2 teaspoon finely grated orange or lemon rind, if liked.

Chocolate Fudge Pudding and Rum Sauce

Preparation time:
  20 minutes
Cooking time:
  1 hour 30 minutes
Serves 4-6

90 g butter
1/2 cup soft brown sugar
3 eggs, separated
1 teaspoon imitation
  vanilla essence
grated rind of 1 orange
1/4 cup milk
1/4 cup orange juice
1 cup self-raising flour
1/4 cup cocoa
1/2 teaspoon
  bicarbonate of soda

Rum Sauce
2 tablespoon soft
  brown sugar
2 tablespoons cocoa
2 tablespoons rum
2 tablespoons butter
1/2 cup cream

1 Preheat oven to moderate 180°C. Brush a 4-cup capacity heatproof bowl or mould with melted butter or oil. Using electric beaters, cream butter and half the sugar in a small mixing bowl until light and creamy. Add egg yolks gradually, beating thoroughly after each addition. Add vanilla essence and rind; beat until combined.
2 Transfer mixture to a large mixing bowl. Combine milk and juice in a jug (the mixture will curdle but won't affect the finished dish). Using a metal spoon, fold in sifted flour, cocoa and soda alternately with milk mixture.
3 Place egg whites in a small, clean, dry mixing bowl. Using electric beaters, beat until stiff peaks form. Add the remaining sugar to the bowl gradually, beating constantly after each addition until sugar is dissolved and the mixture is glossy and thick. Using a metal spoon, fold gently into batter. Pour the mixture into prepared bowl and cover batter with a circle of buttered greaseproof paper, then cover the bowl tightly with foil.
4 Place bowl in a deep, ovenproof dish or baking tray. Add sufficient water to come halfway up the sides of the bowl. Bake for 1 hour 15 minutes. Invert onto a serving platter. Serve warm with Rum Sauce.
5 To make Rum Sauce: Place all ingredients except cream in a pan. Heat, stirring, until smooth. Simmer for 2 minutes, stir in cream.

Classic Baked Egg Custard (top), Chocolate Fudge Pudding and Rum Sauce (bottom).

Rum and Raisin Self-saucing Puddings

Preparation time:
  25 minutes
Cooking time:
  25 minutes
Serves 6

125 g butter
1/2 cup caster sugar
2 eggs, lightly beaten
few drops imitation
  vanilla essence
1 1/2 cups self-raising
  flour
1 tablespoon cocoa
1/3 cup chopped raisins
2 tablespoons milk
1 tablespoon rum
2/3 cup soft brown sugar
1 cup boiling water
2 tablespoons rum, extra

1 Preheat oven to moderate 180°C. Brush 6 x 1-cup capacity ovenproof dishes with melted butter or oil.
2 Using electric beaters, beat butter and sugar in small mixing bowl until light and creamy. Add eggs gradually, beating thoroughly after each addition. Add the vanilla essence, beat until combined. Transfer batter mixture to large mixing bowl. Using a metal spoon, fold in the sifted flour and cocoa alternately with raisins and the combined milk and rum.

3 Spoon into prepared dishes, leaving room for mixture to rise. Combine sugar, water and extra rum. Pour evenly over each pudding. Bake for 25 minutes. To unmould, run a knife around the edge of each pudding. Invert onto serving plates. Serve immediately.

Almond and Apple Pudding with Apricot Sauce

Preparation time:
  15 minutes
Cooking time:
  40 minutes
Serves 4

1/4 cup caster sugar
1 x 800 g can pie apple
90 g butter
1/2 cup caster sugar,
  extra
1 teaspoon grated
  lemon rind
1 tablespoon lemon
  juice
3 eggs, separated
1/2 cup self-raising
  flour
1/2 cup diced almonds

Apricot Sauce
1 cup water
3/4 cup chopped dried
  apricots
1/4 cup caster sugar
2 teaspoons cornflour
juice of 1 lemon

1 Preheat oven to moderate 180°C. Brush a 6-cup capacity ovenproof dish with melted butter or oil. Stir 1/4 cup caster sugar through apple. Spoon apple evenly over base.
2 Using electric beaters, cream butter and extra sugar in a small mixing bowl until light and creamy. Beat in lemon rind, juice, egg yolks, sifted flour and diced almonds until just combined and mixture is almost smooth.
3 Place egg whites in a small, clean, dry mixing bowl. Using electric beaters, beat until stiff peaks form. Using a metal spoon, fold lightly into batter. Spread evenly over apple.
4 Bake for 40 minutes or until lightly browned and the top springs back to the touch. Serve warm or cold with Apricot Sauce.
5 To make Apricot Sauce: Add water and apricots to pan. Bring to the boil; reduce heat. Simmer for 15 minutes; stir in sugar. Remove from heat. Blend the cornflour with lemon juice; stir into apricot mixture. Return to heat. Bring to boil, stirring constantly. Reduce heat and simmer 5 minutes.

Almond and Apple Pudding with Apricot Sauce (top),
Rum and Raisin Self-saucing Pudding (bottom).

Baked Rice Custard

Preparation time:
  20 minutes
Cooking time:
  1 hour
Serves 4

1/4 cup short-grain
  rice
2 eggs, lightly beaten
1/4 cup caster sugar
1/2 cup powdered milk
2 cups water
1 teaspoon imitation
  vanilla essence
1/4 cup sultanas
  (optional)
1 teaspoon ground
  nutmeg

1 Preheat oven to
moderately slow 160°C.
Brush a deep, 20 cm
round ovenproof dish
(1.5 L capacity) with
melted butter or oil .
2 Cook rice in medium
pan of boiling water
until just tender; drain.
Whisk eggs, sugar,
powdered milk, water
and essence in medium
mixing bowl for
2 minutes. Fold in the
cooked rice and the
sultanas. Pour mixture
into prepared dish;
sprinkle with nutmeg.
3 Place filled dish into
a deep baking dish.
Pour in enough cold
water to come halfway
up the sides. Bake for
50 minutes, or until

custard is set and a knife
comes out clean when
inserted in the centre.
Remove dish from the
waterbath immediately.
Leave 5 minutes before
serving with cream.

Lemon-Lime Delicious

Preparation time:
  20 minutes
Cooking time:
  40 minutes
Serves 6

60 g butter
3/4 cup caster sugar
3 eggs, separated
1 teaspoon finely grated
  lemon rind
1 teaspoon finely grated
  lime rind
1/4 cup lemon juice
1/4 cup lime juice
1/3 cup self-raising flour,
  sifted
1 cup milk

1 Preheat oven to
moderate 180°C. Brush
a shallow 6-cup capacity
ovenproof dish with
melted butter or oil.

Using electric beaters,
beat butter and sugar in
small mixing bowl until
light and creamy. Add
egg yolks one at a time,
beating thoroughly
between each addition.
Add lemon and lime
rinds; beat well.
2 Transfer mixture to a
large mixing bowl.
Using a metal spoon,
gently fold in the sifted
flour alternately with
milk. Stir until just
combined. and mixture
is almost smooth.
3 Place egg whites in a
clean, small, dry mixing
bowl. Using electric
beaters, beat until stiff
peaks form. Using a
metal spoon, gently fold
beaten egg whites into
lemon-lime mixture.
4 Pour mixture gently
into prepared dish.
Place filled dish in a
shallow baking dish.
Pour in enough hot
water to come half-way
up the sides. Bake for
40 minutes. Serve
immediately. Decorate
with lemon and lime
slices, if desired. Serve
with whipped cream.

Note: For a different
citrus flavour, try
substituting mandarin,
tangerine, orange, or
plain lemon for the
lemon-lime combination
we used in this recipe.

*Baked Rice Custard (top), Lemon-
Lime Delicious (bottom).*

Bread puddings, crumbles & cobblers

These delicious puddings are based on the combination of soft, baked fruit and crunchy, creamy or cakey toppings. Despite their humble origins, they have a place in every good cook's recipe book because they are easy enough for everyday and firm nursery favourites, yet dress up with alcohol, cream and spices to make very special, grown-up desserts.

❖ ❖ ❖ ❖

Berry Cherry Crumble

Preparation time:
  10 minutes
Cooking time:
  15 minutes
Serves 6

1 x 250 g punnet
  strawberries, hulled
1 x 200 g punnet
  blueberries
1 x 425 g can pitted
  black cherries,
  strained, ¹/2 cup juice
  reserved
¹/2 teaspoon cornflour
1 tablespoon icing sugar

Topping
90 g butter
¹/4 cup golden syrup
2 cups rolled oats

1 Preheat oven to moderate 180°C. Cut strawberries in half. Place in an ovenproof dish with blueberries and cherries. Mix well. Blend cornflour with reserved cherry juice until smooth. Pour over fruit. Sprinkle on sifted icing sugar. Set aside.
2 To prepare Topping: Melt butter and golden syrup in a small pan over low heat. Remove from heat; stir in rolled oats until combined.
3 Spoon the oat mixture over berries. Bake for 15 minutes, or until topping is golden and crunchy. Serve hot.

Note: For extra flavour, add blanched slivered almonds to Topping.

Berry Cherry Crumble (top), Bread and Butter Pudding (bottom).

Bread and Butter Pudding

Preparation time:
  10 minutes
Cooking time:
  50 minutes
Serves 4-6

30 g butter, softened
6 thin slices day-old
  white or brown bread,
  crusts removed
3/4 cup mixed dried fruit
3 tablespoons caster
  sugar
1 teaspoon mixed spice
2 eggs, lightly beaten
1 teaspoon imitation
  vanilla essence
2 1/2 cups milk

1 Preheat oven to
moderate 180°C. Grease
a medium, shallow,
ovenproof dish. Butter
bread and cut the slices
in half diagonally. Layer
bread into the dish,
sprinkling each layer
with dried fruit, sugar
and mixed spice.
2 Beat eggs, essence
and milk together. Pour
over the bread; leave
for 5 minutes to soak.
3 Bake pudding for
50 minutes, or until set
and the top is browned.

Chocolate Rum-Raisin Bread Pudding

Preparation time:
  10 minutes
Cooking time:
  40 minutes
Serves 6

15 g butter, softened
8 slices day-old raisin
  bread, crusts removed
150 g dark chocolate
3/4 cup cream
3 eggs, lightly beaten
1/2 cup caster sugar
1 cup milk
1 tablespoon rum

1 Preheat oven to
moderate 180°C. Brush
a 6-cup capacity
ovenproof dish with
melted butter. Butter
bread. Place, buttered
side up, in prepared dish.
Combine chocolate and
cream in a small pan.
Stir over low heat until
chocolate has melted
and mixture is smooth.
2 Whisk the eggs and
sugar together in a large
mixing bowl, add milk
and chocolate mixture
and beat to combine.
Stir in rum. Pour the
mixture over the bread.
3 Place filled dish in a
baking dish. Pour in
enough hot water to
come half-way up the

sides of the pudding.
Bake for 40 minutes or
until custard is set and
a sharp knife comes out
clean when inserted in
the centre. Serve warm
or cold, with cream.

Note: Use day-old
bread, as fresh bread
may make become soggy.

Apricot Betty

Preparation time:
  10 minutes
Cooking time:
  30 minutes
Serves 6

2 x 425 g cans apricot
  halves, drained, 1/3
  cup juice reserved
1/4 cup caster sugar
2 cups/120 g fine, fresh
  white breadcrumbs
50 g butter, melted

1 Preheat oven to
moderate 180°C. Brush
a 20 cm pie dish with
melted butter. Place half
the apricots into the
prepared dish.
2 Sprinkle with half the
caster sugar and half
the breadcrumbs. Pour
half the butter and half
the juice over crumbs.
3 Repeat with the
remaining ingredients.
Bake for 30 minutes.
Serve hot with the sauce
of your choice.

*Chocolate Rum-Raisin Bread Pudding (top),
Apricot Betty (bottom).*

1. *For Caramel Banana Pudding: Cut sliced bread into rectangles.*

2. *Pour egg mixture over cubed banana and sliced bread in dish.*

Caramel Banana Pudding

Preparation time:
  20 minutes
Cooking time:
  45 minutes
Serves 6

30 g butter, softened
6 slices day-old white
  bread, crusts
  removed
2 large bananas,
  peeled and cut into
  1 cm cubes
2 tablespoons soft
  brown sugar
1 tablespoon malted
  milk powder
1 tablespoon caramel
  corn syrup
3 eggs, lightly beaten
3/4 cup cream
1 cup milk
1 tablespoon malted
  milk powder, extra
1 tablespoon soft
  brown sugar, extra

1 Preheat oven to moderate 180°C. Brush a shallow, 8-cup capacity, rectangular ovenproof dish with melted butter or oil. Butter the bread and cut 3 slices into rectangles to line base of dish. Place banana on top.
2 Combine sugar, milk powder, syrup, eggs, cream and milk in a medium bowl. Whisk until well combined. Pour mixture over banana and bread.
3 Cut remaining bread into 2 cm cubes. Place in a bowl with extra milk powder and sugar, stir and sprinkle over pudding. Bake for 45 minutes or until custard is set and a sharp knife comes out clean when inserted in the centre. Serve hot or cold with cream. This pudding must be eaten the day it is made.

Caramel Banana Pudding.

3. *Place cubed bread in a bowl with milk powder and sugar. Stir to combine.*

4. *Custard is set when a knife inserted in the centre comes out clean.*

Raspberry Bread Pudding

Preparation time:
  10 minutes
Cooking time:
  50 minutes
Serves 6

30 g butter, softened
6-8 slices day-old white
  bread, crusts removed
300 g frozen
  raspberries, thawed
3 eggs, lightly beaten
1/2 cup caster sugar
1 3/4 cups milk
2 tablespoons whisky

1 Preheat oven to
moderate 180°C. Brush a
6-cup capacity ovenproof
dish with melted butter.
Butter bread and slice in
half diagonally. Arrange
a third of the bread,
buttered side up, on the
base of the prepared
dish. Cover with half the
raspberries. Repeat layers
finishing with bread.
2 Whisk eggs and sugar
together, add milk and
beat to combine. Stir in
whisky. Pour over bread.
3 Place filled dish in a
baking dish. Pour in hot
water to come half-way
up the sides of pudding.
Bake for 50 minutes or
until custard is set and
a sharp knife comes out
clean. Serve warm.

Spiced Plum Crumble

Preparation time:
  10 minutes
Cooking time:
  15 minutes
Serves 6

1 x 825 g can dark
  plums, drained, pitted
1/4 cup soft brown sugar
1 teaspoon cornflour
1 tablespoon brandy
2 teaspoon grated
  orange rind
2 tablespoons orange
  juice

Topping
1 cup toasted muesli
2 tablespoon plain flour
45 g butter, melted

1 Preheat oven to
moderate 180°C. Place
the plums in a shallow
ovenproof dish.
2 In a small bowl mix
sugar, cornflour, brandy,
orange rind and juice
together until smooth;
pour over the plums and
stir through.
3 To make Topping:
Combine muesli and
sifted flour in a bowl;
stir in the butter. Spoon
evenly over plums. Bake
for 15 minutes, or until
topping is golden. Serve
hot with whipped
cream or ice-cream.

*Raspberry Bread Pudding (top), Spiced
Plum Crumble (bottom).*

Peach and Pineapple Coconut Crumble

Preparation time:
  10 minutes
Cooking time:
  20 minutes
Serves 6

1 x 825 g can peach
  halves
1 x 450 g can pineapple
  pieces
2 tablespoons orange
  marmalade
1 teaspoon rum

Topping
1 cup/90 g dried
  breadcrumbs
2 tablespoons plain
  flour
1/3 cup shredded coconut
90 g butter
1 tablespoon honey

1 Preheat oven to moderate 180°C. Drain fruits, reserving a total of 1 cup of juice. Place fruit in a shallow ovenproof dish.
2 Combine reserved juice, marmalade and rum over low heat in a small pan. Bring to the boil, reduce heat and simmer, uncovered, until mixture is a thick syrup; this will take about 5 minutes. Pour over the fruit.

3 To make Topping: Mix together the breadcrumbs, sifted flour and shredded coconut in a bowl. Heat butter and honey in a small pan until melted; stir into dry ingredients until combined. Spoon mixture over fruit. Bake for 20 minutes, or until topping is golden. Serve warm with custard.

Dried Fruit Cobbler

Preparation time:
  20 minutes
Cooking time:
  20 minutes
Serves 6

500 g mixed dried fruit,
  chopped
2 cups hot water
1/3 cup soft brown sugar
1/2 teaspoon cinnamon
1/4 teaspoon ground
  ginger
1/4 teaspoon ground
  cloves

Topping
2 cups self-raising flour
1 teaspoon baking
  powder
50 g butter, chopped
1 tablespoon caster
  sugar
3/4 cup milk
milk, extra
soft brown sugar, extra

1 Preheat oven to moderate 180°C. Brush a 22 cm, 6-cup capacity ovenproof dish with melted butter. Soak dried fruit in hot water for 10 minutes. Drain well; mix sugar and spices through and spoon into prepared dish. Cover with aluminium foil and place in oven while you prepare the Topping.
2 To make Topping: Sift flour and baking powder into large mixing bowl. Using fingertips, rub butter into flour until the mixture is a fine, crumbly texture; stir in sugar. Add almost all the liquid, mix to a soft dough, adding more liquid if necessary. Turn onto a floured surface, and knead for 2 minutes or until smooth.
3 Roll dough out to 1 cm thickness. Using a 5 cm round cutter, cut out about 17 rounds. Remove dish from oven and uncover. Arrange rounds of dough on top of fruit, brush with a little milk and sprinkle lightly with sugar. Return to oven bake for 20 minutes. Serve warm.

Note: Fruit mixture must be hot when the dough rounds are placed over it or the cobbler dough will not cook completely.

Peach and Pineapple Coconut Crumble (top),
Dried Fruit Cobbler (bottom).

Peach and Pear Betty

Preparation time:
  15 minutes
Cooking time:
  15 minutes
Serves 4-6

1 x 425 g can peach
  slices, drained, 1/4 cup
  juice reserved
1 x 425 g can pear
  halves, drained,
  1/4 cup juice reserved
30 g butter, softened
2 slices white bread,
  crusts removed
2 slices wholegrain
  bread, crusts removed
1 teaspoon ground
  cinnamon
1/4 teaspoon ground
  ginger
2 tablespoons soft dark
  brown sugar
1/2 cup slivered almonds
1 tablespoon honey

1 Preheat oven to
moderate 180°C.
Brush a shallow, 20 cm
round ovenproof dish
(4-cup capacity) with
melted butter.
2 Arrange the peaches
and pears in the base of
the dish; pour over
combined juices. Butter
the bread slices.
3 Using a 2 cm cutter,
cut out rounds from the
bread. Place the bread
rounds, cinnamon,
ginger, brown sugar and
almonds in a medium

mixing bowl. Stir until
well combined. Spoon
mixture over fruit and
drizzle honey over. Bake
for 15 minutes, or until
fruit is hot and topping
is browned and crunchy.
Serve immediately.

Apple Nut Cobbler

Preparation time:
  25 minutes
Cooking time:
  35 minutes
Serves 8

4 large green apples,
  peeled, cut into
  12 wedges
1/4 cup fig jam
1 tablespoon lemon
  juice

Batter
2 eggs, lightly beaten
2 tablespoons soft
  brown sugar
1 tablespoon golden
  syrup
1 tablespoon fig jam
1/4 cup buttermilk
50 g butter, melted
100 g honey-roasted
  peanuts, coarsely
  ground
1/3 cup self-raising flour

Topping
50 g honey-roasted
  peanuts, coarsely
  ground
2 tablespoons soft
  brown sugar

1 Preheat oven to
moderate 180°C. Brush
a shallow, 8-cup
capacity rectangular
ovenproof dish with
melted butter or oil.
2 Arrange apples over
the base of the dish.
Combine jam and juice
in a small pan. Stir over
low heat until jam has
melted; remove from
heat. Pour over apples.
Bake 15 minutes or
until apple is hot.
3 Using electric beaters,
beat eggs in a small
mixing bowl for
5 minutes or until thick
and pale. Add sugar
gradually, beating
constantly until
dissolved and mixture is
pale golden and glossy;
add syrup, beat until
combined. Transfer
mixture to large mixing
bowl. Using a metal
spoon, fold in jam,
buttermilk, butter,
peanuts and sifted flour
quickly and lightly.
4 Spoon the mixture
evenly over hot apple,
smooth surface and
sprinkle combined
Topping ingredients
over batter. Bake for
20 minutes or until a
skewer comes out clean
when inserted in centre.

Note: Spoon the batter
over hot fruit or it will
not cook completely.

*Apple Nut Cobbler (top), Peach
and Pear Betty (bottom).*

Spiced Rhubarb and Pear Cobbler

Preparation time:
  25 minutes
Cooking time:
  35 minutes
Serves 4

400 g fresh rhubarb
3 large pears, peeled
1 tablespoon finely
  grated orange rind
1 tablespoon finely
  grated lemon rind
1/2 teaspoon mixed spice
1/3 cup demerara sugar
2 tablespoons marsala
2 tablespoons orange
  juice

Batter
1/3 cup self-raising flour
2 tablespoons plain flour
1/4 cup desiccated
  coconut
2 tablespoons caster
  sugar
2 eggs, lightly beaten
2 tablespoons milk
25 g butter, melted

Topping
1 cup fresh white
  breadcrumbs
1/2 cup demerara sugar
4 tablespoons desiccated
  or shredded coconut
60 g butter, melted

1 Preheat oven to moderate 180°C. Brush a deep, 6-cup capacity rectangular ovenproof dish with melted butter or oil.
2 Wash the rhubarb, cut into 3 cm cubes. Cut pears into 2 cm cubes. Combine the rhubarb, pears, orange and lemon rind, mixed spice, demerara sugar, marsala and orange juice in a large pan. Cover and simmer for 10 minutes, stirring occasionally. Remove from heat. Keep warm.
3 To make Batter: Sift the flour, coconut and caster sugar into a medium mixing bowl;

make a well in the centre. Add combined egg, milk and butter all at once. Whisk until all liquid is incorporated and batter is smooth and free of lumps.
4 Pour hot fruit into prepared dish. Pour batter evenly over the top. For Topping, combine breadcrumbs, sugar, coconut and butter in a small mixing bowl. Sprinkle over batter. Bake the cobbler for 25 minutes or until skewer comes out clean when inserted in centre. Serve immediately.

HINT
For a special dessert, make a rich bread pudding using cream, brioche and fruit soaked in rum or orange liqueur. Serve chilled, with brandy or whisky custard.

Spiced Rhubarb and Pear Cobbler.

1. For Spiced Rhubarb and Pear Cobbler: Wash rhubarb, cut into 3 cm cubes.

2. Simmer fruit, stirring occasionally. Remove from heat and keep warm.

3. Make a well in the centre of the flour and add combined egg, milk and butter

4. Pour hot fruit into prepared dish. Pour batter evenly over the top.

For brew freaks, bean geeks and the simply curious, the first *Ireland Independent Coffee Guide* reveals over **130 of the best speciality coffee shops and roasters**, hand-picked by leading coffee experts.

Join the **speciality coffee revolution** and discover artisan beans of the highest quality which are being **roasted in Ireland** and crafted into outstanding brews by a band of top-notch **independent coffee shops**.

DISCOVER THE BEST COFFEE IN IRELAND

WWW.INDYCOFFEE.GUIDE

🐦 @indycoffeeguide   📷 indycoffeeguide

food
insider's guide

A food Insider's Guide, published by Salt Media. www.saltmedia.co.uk

£7.99 | €9.99

ISBN 978-0-9955493-3-3

9 780995 549333

salt media

Index